THE SOCIETY FOR THE SCIENTIFIC STUDY OF SEX

A BRIEF HISTORY

Vern L. Bullough

A Publication of

THE FOUNDATION FOR THE
SCIENTIFIC STUDY OF SEXUALITY

P.O. Box 208 • Mt. Vernon, IA 52314

Printed by
Graphic Publishing Company
Lake Mills, Iowa

THE SOCIETY FOR THE SCIENTIFIC STUDY OF SEX

Mission Statement

The Society for the Scientific Study of Sex is dedicated to advancing knowledge of sexuality. To acquire that knowledge the Society requires freedom of inquiry, support for research, and an interdisciplinary network of collaborating scholars. The Society believes in the importance of both the production of quality research and the application of sexual knowledge in educational, clinical, and other settings. The Society also sees as essential the communication of accurate information about sexuality to professionals, policy makers, and the general public.

Scientific knowledge of sexuality forms the foundation for all professional services in sexuality. This knowledge is different from opinion, requiring the collection and interpretation of evidence using public, universal, and critical scholarly standards. To this end, the Society fosters a world-wide, interdisciplinary community for professionals who, regardless of their specialization, are committed to a serious, scholarly, and scientific approach to acquiring and disseminating knowledge of sexuality. The Society provides a forum for communication, collaboration, and critical evaluation among sexuality professionals.

The Society is also dedicated to promoting human welfare by reducing ignorance and prejudice about sexuality. Science illuminates sexuality; joined with wisdom and compassion, it enhances the quality of lives.

i

THE FOUNDATION FOR THE SCIENTIFIC STUDY OF SEXUALITY

Mission Statement

The Foundation for the Scientific Study of Sexuality (FSSS) was created for the purpose of stimulating and supporting scholarly research-related activities in the area of sexuality. The primary goal of FSSS is to make available a perpetual pool of funds to facilitate the accomplishment of this purpose. The funds may be regranted to organizations and individuals, and FSSS may operate its own programs.

The Foundation was created by the Society for the Scientific Study of Sex (SSSS), a professional membership organization of researchers and scholars devoted to a scientific approach to understanding sexuality. SSSS was formed in 1957. FSSS was created to address the need for financial support for high quality, scientific research in this field and in response to the paucity of existing support for such research. No other foundation devoted exclusively or primarily to supporting scientific research in sexuality exists. Foundation, government, and corporate support for basic sexuality research always has been limited, and, in recent years, it has declined. When funding has existed, usually it has been linked with a major crisis in the society, such as AIDS.

Serious research in sexuality has been carried on for several decades. Routinely, that research has been hampered by inadequate funding. The result is that progress toward understanding has been slowed, and the quality of the work has sometimes suffered. FSSS will address these problems by providing financial assistance to researchers for activities such as the following: the development of research proposals for submission to other funding agencies; the conducting of research; the dissemination of research findings; specialized research training; specialized research seminars, colloquia, or conferences; scholarships; and awards for excellence in research.

Although independently incorporated, FSSS will retain close links with SSSS, its Board of Directors being appointed, in part, from the Directors of SSSS. Consistent with SSSS's more than 30 year history of successful, cost-effective service to its membership, the FSSS leadership will exhibit the same commitment to excellence and productivity. In so doing it will be successful in producing an endowment that will be a major continuing force fostering the advancement of sexual science. Its leadership and staff are entirely volunteers. All contributions to FSSS are used to further the mission of the Foundation.

For further information about the Foundation, contact Howard J. Ruppel, Jr., Executive Director, P.O. Box 208, Mt. Vernon, IA 52314.

Preface

This book is an extension of a paper presented at the 30th Annual Meeting of the Society for the Scientific Study of Sex, in Atlanta, Georgia, on November 8, 1987. That paper was entitled "Sex Research and the Place of the Society for the Scientific Study of Sex." The portions of the book dealing with the history of the Society for the Scientific Study of Sex are based upon interviews, responses from past presidents to an initial draft, and archive materials either in their hands or mine. When quotation marks are used, it is a verbatim statement or copy of a statement from these materials.

Acknowledgements

I would like to thank all of the past presidents of the Society for the information they provided about the history of the Society and their roles in it.

I would also like to thank Sandra L. and Clive M. Davis for their assistance in editing the manuscript, and Howard J. and Barbara Wiedemann Ruppel for their financial support of its publication.

This book is published by **The Foundation for the Scientific Study of Sexuality**, the fund-raising and research-supporting organization created by **The Society for the Scientific Study of Sex.**

Contents

The 30th Anniversary of SSSS

In 1987, The Society for the Scientific Study of Sex (SSSS) was 30 years old. For professional societies, this is not particularly old, but since it has survived longer than any other organized group of professionals working in human sexuality, this represented an important milestone in the history of sexology. This publication represents an attempt to place the Society in its historical setting and to give information about sex research in the United States, primarily through the perspective of the past presidents of the Society. (See Appendix 1.)

Organizing any new professional society is a difficult task. Organizing one which took as its purview the study of sexuality, what might euphemistically be called a "delicate topic," raised special problems. Still, 30 years ago, there were special benefits for the membership, namely a feeling of togetherness which overcame the scholarly isolation felt by so many researchers and professionals in the field; a reinforcement of the belief that they were doing something important; and a chance to explore new frontiers with others of like interest and to receive the benefit of their critical examination. Almost everyone who affiliated with the Society in its early years mentioned the problem of isolation and lack of understanding from colleagues outside of the sex field as a reason for coming together.

Though sex research had been conducted in this country since the turn of the century, those few scholars willing to identify themselves as sex researchers looked to Europe for support and affiliation. In fact, in the 1920s, when the Rockefeller Foundation first offered financial support for sex research, the scientists involved made a conscious effort to avoid organizing as a society of sex researchers or even identifying themselves as sex researchers, let alone publishing a journal devoted to sex research. One of the major reasons for this appears to have been the fear that mainstream society would denigrate them and their research if it was somehow labeled as sex research. Scientists were also worried that they might not be regarded as professionals if they dealt with sex, a subject believed to belong to the radical reformer and not to the true researcher (Bullough, 1985a).

Sex Research in the 19th Century

Modern sex research began with the study of prostitution by Alexander Jean Baptiste Parent-Duchatelet (1790-1836). He gathered information about the 3,558 registered prostitutes of Paris (he excluded clandestine, part-time, and amateur prostitutes) and found that the inscribed (those whose names were inscribed on a register) prostitute was in her late teens or early twenties, illiterate, poor, probably illegitimate or from a broken family, and likely to have regarded herself as a prostitute for a relatively brief period (Parent-Duchatelet, 1837). Prostitution continued to be a major area of study, and, in fact, American sex research received a strong impetus from such studies. It was the study of prostitution, for example, which first aroused the interest of John D. Rockefeller, Jr., in sex research (Bullough, 1985a, 1988).

Another early area of research was in contraception, culminating in the last part of the 19th century with the invention of the diaphragm by Mensinga and the development of the early spermaticides, as well as the appearance of the rubber condom (Bullough, 1980; 1981). Americans played a lesser role in these developments in large part because of the difficulty in disseminating information about contraceptives. Not until early in the 20th century when some of the barriers had been eliminated did Americans enter the field.

Overshadowing both of these areas during the last part of the 19th century and first part of the 20th was the growing concern with sexually transmitted diseases, particularly syphilis, the stages of which had finally been described at the end of the 19th century. The discovery of the sequellae of the third stage of syphilis led to the realization that many of the diseases previously attributed simply to an active sexual life were, in fact, due to a disease. This ultimately led to changes in attitudes toward sex itself. Further assisting in this change was the discovery in 1905 of Treponema pallidum (by Shaudinn and Hoffman) as well as other bacteria responsible for additional sexually transmitted disease. These discoveries were soon followed by a search for a cure, and, though various cures did develop, it was not until the development of antibiotics such as penicillin that complete cures were realized.

Gender studies were also important in the last part of the 19th century as women mounted an effective challenge to traditional viewpoints of women's role and the limitations of female biology. The first generation of feminists had to fight not only the legal and economic bias and the traditional religious emphasis on the subordination of women, but also the science of the time emphasizing the inferiority of the female. Some physicians even regarded menstruation as a pathological phenomenon, "proving" such inferiority (Bullough, 1976, 1985b; Bullough, Shelton, & Slavin, 1988). This encouraged feminists, as well as others, to do research into sex and gender. Karl Pearson, an English eugenicist, for example, held that questions about women's role and place in society could not really be answered until a new science of "sexualogy" took shape, providing answers to questions about female biology and sexuality (Pearson, 1888).

Germany and Sex Research

Suddenly, variant forms of sexuality, previously grouped together as the sin against nature, received attention and publicity (Krafft-Ebing, 1894). Giving impetus to these attempts of the medical and legal community to describe variant forms of sexual behavior was the organized effort of homosexuals and their supporters in Germany to avoid having homosexual behavior classified as criminal. Late 19th century Germany was emerging as a new nation, incorporating a large number of separate German-speaking countries and cities under Prussian leadership. Many of these independent governmental units had followed the Napoleonic code, a code not so much concerned with kinds of sexual variations as was with consent and protection for certain groups (e.g., children). In Prussia, however, homosexual activity was itself a criminal activity and it was feared that the new German state would adopt the Prussian code rather than the more liberal code prevailing in much of Germany. This led many homosexuals as well as liberal reformers to agitate publicly against the adoption of the Prussian code. When such agitation proved unsuccessful, the movement continued its efforts to change the law. What started as a political movement soon turned into an effort to understand homosexuality and other forms of stigmatized behavior. This led to the first efforts to coordinate sex research and brought Germany to the leadership of the movement for sex research (Bullough, 1988b).

Most of the people working in sex research originally did so from within a very narrow disciplinary approach and did not regard themselves as sexuality researchers but as virologists, cytologists, gynecologists, or urologists. A few, however, began to see the limitations of their own specialty and the need to share information across disciplines. Germany and German-speaking areas served as the focal point for many of these interdisciplinary investigators who laid the foundation for sexology. Among the early German investigators were Richard von Krafft-Ebing (1840-1902), Iwan Bloch (1872-1922), Magnus Hirschfeld (1868-1935), Albert Moll (1862-1939), and Carl F.D. Westphal (1833-1890). In the Austrian-Hungarian empire, Sigmund Freud, though a participant in the German sexological movement, remained independent of it.

One result was the appearance of specialized journals devoted to sexology. The first, started in 1899, was the *Jahrbuch für Sexuelle Zwischenstufen* devoted to the study of homosexuality. This was followed by a more generalized journal, *Zeitschrift für Sexualwissenschaft*, which included in its first issues articles by such individuals as Sigmund Freud, Alfred Adler, Paolo Mantegazza, Cesare Lombroso, Wilhelm Stekel, and Magnus Hirschfeld. The plans were more ambitious than the times and, after the first year, the journal was combined with a more popular journal, *Sexual Probleme*, and issued under the title of *Zeitschrift für Sexualwissenschaft und Sexual Politik*. The organizing force behind much of this was Magnus Hirschfeld who originally had started with studies of homosexuality but soon expanded into studies of sexuality and marriage in general. Hirschfeld established an Institute for Sexual Science which included a marriage consultation department providing advice on the problems of contraception, frigidity, and impotence, and, through lectures and discussion, offered a popular educational program on various sexual topics (Bullough, 1988b).

Though the German scholars collectively dominated the field, they were not alone. In fact, the dominant figure in the English speaking world, and certainly in the United States, was Havelock Ellis whose studies, in what he ultimately called the *Psychology of Sex*, awakened interest in sexual studies throughout the English speaking world (Ellis, 1936). It is worthy of note that Ellis's first study, on homosexuality, was published in German, an indication of the greater willingness of researchers in Germany at that time to examine sexual issues.

The First Congresses

As the number of sex researchers grew, professional groups also emerged. The first such group was the Society of Physicians for Sexual Science and Eugenics founded in Berlin in 1913 by Magnus Hirschfeld and Albert Eulenburg. This was almost immediately countered in that same year by another group, the International Society for Sexual Research organized by Albert Moll. Each organization strove to consolidate itself by organizing an international congress, efforts which were handicapped by the outbreak of World War I. It was not until 1921 that Hirschfeld and his allies managed to hold, in Berlin, the **International Congress for Sexual Reform on a Sexological Basis**. This was one of the first international congresses of any kind to be held in Germany after World War I. His organizing committee included scientists from Tokyo, Beijing, Moscow, Copenhagen, London, Rome and San Francisco. The Congress had 28 papers in four major areas: (1) sexual endocrinology, (2) sex and the law, (3) birth control, and (4) sex education. The Congress ended with a call for legal and social reform, and it was this effort for reform, more than the program, that engendered criticism. The reforms urged, however, seem modest today: dissemination of contraceptives, freedom to divorce, change in marriage laws regarding women, effective sex education, etc.

In 1926, Moll and his group countered with a far more impressive meeting, the **International Congress for Sex Research**, also held in Berlin. The meeting covered roughly the same areas as Hirschfeld's earlier congress but offered nearly three times as many speakers. Hirschfeld followed his 1922 congress with one in Copenhagen in 1928, and out of this came the World League for Sexual Reform with Hirschfeld, August Forel, and Havelock Ellis as co-presidents. This organization seemed as much political as sexological. It sponsored the next three congresses, in London in 1929 (organized by Norman Haire), in Vienna in 1930, and in Brno, Czechloslovakia in 1932.

The league had a rather stormy history mainly because of disputes among its members over sexual reform in the Soviet Union. The split revolved around the question of whether it was necessary to reform society before sexual reform could take place or whether it was worthwhile to agitate for sexual reform even in an unreformed society. In the 1930s, one of the League's presidents, J.H. Leunbach insisted it be affiliated with the revolutionary worker's movement, whereas the other, Norman Haire, was determined to keep all revolutionary activity out of the League by emphasizing the need to concentrate on education. It was not the disputes, however, which gave the death knell to the international organization but the rise of the Nazis and their destruction of the German sexological movement (Bullough, 1988b).

Norman Haire attempted through his writings and organizational skills, to keep his wing of the society alive. Two British organizations emerged, the Sex Education Society, and the British Society for the Study of Sexual Psychology. Haire also edited a journal associated with the first group, the *Journal of Sex Education* but with his death in 1952 the journal ended. Also working to keep some international cooperation going was the Indian sex researcher, A.P. Pillay who edited the *International Journal of Sexology* from 1947-55, a successor to an earlier journal he had started entitled *Marriage Hygiene*. There were also various birth control organizations, both national and international, which continued to exist, but with the death of Haire and Pillay any semblance of a professional organization devoted to sexology (as distinct from contraception) on either the national or international level no longer existed.

American Entry into the Field

Though some Americans had participated in the European congresses, sex research had remained a more or less individual endeavor except for the American Social Hygiene Association, an organization formed by the merging of various purity groups including, on the one hand, the American Purity Alliance and the American Vigilance Committee, and on the other hand, the American Federation for Sex Hygiene (originally the American Society of Sanitary and Moral Prophylaxis). The primary purpose of these groups, as well as the American Social Hygiene Association, was to eliminate prostitution and educate the young about the dangers of venereal disease. Still, it was the Bureau of Social Hygiene, the research arm of the American Social Hygiene Association, that served as the sponsor for much of the sex research taking place in the United States from 1913 to 1930 (Bullough, 1985a; 1988a). Although this research was important, particularly the prostitution and hormonal studies, both the intent and the subject matter was different from the research associated with the emerging sexology movement on the continent.

Americans, however, also contributed significant research in some of the areas of sexual behavior that had been emphasized by the Europeans. Havelock Ellis briefly surveyed American sex research in 1931 and, in the process, summarized the difficulties with sex research in general. He explained that modern sex research owed its origins to German investigators and, although others had followed, their investigations had failed to result in any wide-scale study of "normal" sexuality in any methodically statistical forms which may lead to fruitful conclusions and definite progress. An investigation of sex activities and sex relationships among fairly normal people, on a sufficiently large and systematic scale to be treated statistically, is quite new, and the most carefully conducted and most illuminating studies, as we may probably consider them, have been carried out ... by American investigators who have worked among the people of the United States. (Dickinson & Beam, 1931, p. vii)

Ellis mentioned three American researchers, Katherine Bement Davis, Robert Latou Dickinson, and Gilbert V. Hamilton as particularly significant (Davis, 1929; Hamilton, 1929; Dickinson and Beam, 1931). Although Dickinson's studies were based on data he had collected in his years of practice as an gynecological specialist, both Davis and Hamilton were supported by the Rockefeller Foundation. This emerging leadership of the Americans in the field of sex research and the emphasis on statistics was consolidated during the Second World War and immediately following it by the research of Alfred Kinsey (Kinsey, Pomeroy, Martin, 1949; Kinsey, Pomeroy, Martin, Gebhard, 1953). Kinsey also was supported by the Rockefeller Foundation. Americans in this same period had taken the leadership in endocrinological and contraceptive research, again largely through Rockefeller support (Bullough, 1985).

Perhaps the first organization in which some sex researchers could be recognized as professionals was the National Council on Family Relations. This organization had been established in 1939 and, with it, the journal, *Living*, later known as the *Journal of Marriage and the Family*. Sex within marriage was regarded as a significant content area by professionals in the field, and some aspects of sexual behavior, particularly as they related to courtship and marriage were incorporated into the college curriculum either in sociology, home economics, or psychology courses (Broderick, 1988; Thurston, 1932). For the most part, however, *Living*, at least in its early years, avoided dealing with sexual issues directly.

Giving further impetus to sexology in the United States was the influx of refugees, particularly from Nazi Germany, including Hans Lehfeldt, one of the founders of the Society for the Scientific Study of Sex. The most significant factor in changing attitudes and making sex research respectable, however, was the publication of the Kinsey reports (Kinsey et al., 1948, 1953). These studies made the United States the new center of sex research.

Inevitably, both because of the number of native born American sex researchers and the number of refugee experts from Europe, Americans were placed in an unique position to take the leadership in any postwar organization of sex professionals. Moreover, many of the Americans engaged in sex research or sex education felt a real need for some kind of organization. In fact, many of those interviewed for this paper, as well as those who over the years have recorded some aspects of their past in the *pentimento* series organized by Leah Schaefer, have emphasized the emotional needs met by the group support provided by fellow professionals.

Because numbers were small and widely scattered, only in a few cities could group support occur on a local level; for most, until fairly recently, it could only come from a national organization.

The Beginnings of the SSSS

The person who took the initial step in this direction was Albert Ellis. Ellis formulated the name, the Society for the Scientific Study of Sex, in 1950, and tried to organize a society. He failed at first. The failure might be explained simply by saying the times were not propitious for the establishment of such a group, but in fact, Ellis might have succeeded if it had not been for the opposition of Alfred Kinsey. Whether Kinsey was fearful that such an organization might compete for funds with his own research institute, as some have said, or whether, having studied the history of the European groups, he was fearful of having sex researchers involved in campaigning for sexual reforms and thus endangering his funds, is not clear. The failure of the initial effort did not discourage Ellis who kept the idea and the name alive.

Giving a renewed impetus to organization was Hans Lehfeldt. Lehfeldt had been encouraged by his friend Norman Haire, shortly before Haire's death, to contact Albert Ellis and Henry Guze about the establishment of some sort of sexological society in the United States. In 1957 the three of them joined with Robert Sherwin, a lawyer, and Hugo Beigel, a psychologist, to lay the groundwork for a society. Harry Benjamin lent his support to the group but did not take an active role in planning programs. The organizing group drew up a constitution stating that the purpose of the proposed society was to

(a) unite in common organization those professionally engaged in various disciplines ... who are similarly engaged in the conducting of sexual research or whose profession involves issues relating to sex ....

(b) to hold periodic scientific meetings for the presentation of research papers and to organize symposia, seminars, workshops, and conferences to consider all aspects of sexuality.

(c) to publish a scientific journal ... and a newsletter ... and other separate publications.

(d) to create a central source for those seeking research information in the field of sex science. (See page i for the current version of the Society's Mission Statement.)

The first year was devoted to extending the membership, something that did not prove easy. Guze, a professor of psychology at Long Island University, wrote a letter to many of his colleagues stating that the time had come to organize a society for sexual research. Others wrote similar letters but recruitment was not easy. Christopher Tietze, the population control expert, who became the second president of the SSSS, initially indicated that he felt he could "not stretch the tolerance of my hospital still further by embarking upon another unorthodox venture." Margaret Sanger was willing to serve on the Advisory Board of the SSSS but wrote that she declined to become a charter member because she needed to concentrate "on the one cause nearest to my heart, the International Planned Parenthood Federation."[1]

Ultimately, some 47 professionals were found who were willing to be listed as charter members (See Appendix 2). In spite of the distinguished list of charter members, formal incorporation proved difficult to secure, perhaps because of the use of the term *sex* in the title. It was not until 1965 that the SSSS was formally incorporated in New York State, and this was done largely through the efforts of the attorney Milton Bergerman. When the SSSS did incorporate it did so as a 501(c)(3) organization, that is, a charitable organization to advance a cause, in this case sexual science, rather than a 501(c)(4), an organization of professionals designed to advance the interest of its members. Unfortunately, the reason for this is not now known by any of the surviving charter members, but it does make SSSS different from most professional groups because the basis of its existence is not to advance its members but rather to advance the entire field of sexual science.

Lack of incorporation, however, did not halt the activities of the organizing group. A kick-off conference of the new society was held on Saturday, November 8, 1958. Sessions were devoted to therapeutic abortion and frigidity. It is from this conference that the SSSS dates its foundation.

The organizing group continued to meet and began a policy of holding an annual, all-day conference in the fall, along with a series of public meetings on various topics. These meetings were usually held at the Barbizon Plaza Hotel on Sunday evenings at 8:30 p.m. either bimonthly or quarterly. Minutes about what took place are not always available, and recollections of early members are sometimes vague.

Formal Organization of SSSS

It was not until 1960 that the Society finally got around to electing officers: One of the reasons for the delay was the conflict between Hans Lehfeldt and Albert Ellis. For a time Lehfeldt threatened to resign if Albert Ellis, who had been elected the first president, took office. Lehfeldt feared that Ellis was too controversial. Parenthetically, a fear of controversy and notoriety was something that many of those engaged in sex research and education at the time tried to avoid. A.P. Pillay, for example, refused to publish Ellis' article, "New Light on Masturbation," in his journal because it was too outspoken. Lehfeldt ultimately was persuaded to change his mind by Henry Guze, allowing Albert Ellis to assume office as the first president in 1960 with Christopher Tietze, the friend and candidate of Lehfeldt, as President-Elect. Robert V. Sherwin served as treasurer and Hugo Beigel was secretary. As secretary, Beigel also edited the newsletter of the Society which usually appeared several weeks before the Sunday evening meeting. The constitution was not ratified until shortly before the 4th annual fall conference in 1961, although those not attending that meeting did not learn of the ratification until a year later when the December, 1962, *Newsletter* reported the vote. Some 91 votes were cast: 87 approved of the constitution, 3 disapproved, and 1 approved with specific reservations.

In the early years, Ellis was the most publicly known individual in the Society. His willingness to speak out on issues which Americans, in general, were hesitant to mention brought him considerable notoriety. Others in the SSSS were reluctant to seek publicity because inevitably they feared it would be adverse publicity. Caution was, perhaps, advisable, for it was in 1960, just as Ellis was set to take the presidency, that an Assistant Professor at the University of Illinois, Leo F. Koch, was dismissed for writing about sex in the *Daily Illini*. Koch wrote a letter responding to an article on "Sex Ritualized" by two male students complaining about the smooching, petting, and "passionate murmuring" taking place late at night in the fraternity and sorority houses, emphasizing that the social pressure on girls [their term] was such that men [their term] were not concerned with "girls as a living unit but as a simple female sex unit."

Koch had responded to this with a letter stating that the basic problem was that sex was a forbidden subject. Men, accustomed to the double standard, could not discuss sex openly with women without regarding them as somehow depraved. He argued that, with the availability of contraceptives, there was no valid reason why individuals with sufficient maturity could not engage in sexual intercourse if they agreed to do so. He concluded that what the authors were complaining about was society imposed silliness.

Though Albert Ellis had said similar things in his books, this letter caused Koch's dismissal (AAUP, 1963). With the efforts of the SSSS to keep a low profile, even to the extent of requiring prospective members to go through an investigative procedure and board approval for membership, it seems clear that the notoriety surrounding Ellis at this time over his outspokenness on sexual issues made Lehfeldt fearful the Society was communicating the wrong message to the public. In short, some of the same issues which had troubled the sex field earlier continued to appear with the founding of the American groups, namely the question of whether sex reform (in terms of communication of research results) can be separated from sex research, and what role a professional society of sexologists should play. With the selection of Ellis the society demonstrated that it was important to convey the findings to the public.

Ellis was a symbolic first president in other ways because he also served as a significant bridge with some of our predecessors in the field of sexology. He knew Pillay, the Indian sexologist, serving as coeditor of the Indian journal with him as well as publishing books with him. He also knew Norman Haire who had written a forward to the British edition of *The Folklore of Sex*, published in London under the title of *Sex Beliefs and Customs* (Ellis, 1952). At this time, Ellis was almost as well known to the general public for his writings about sex as Kinsey.

Because so much of the burden of running the SSSS fell either on the president or the president-elect (who acted as program chair), much of the history of the society during its formative years is dependent upon what the president did. Because support services in the society were nonexistent or minimal, the president often also had to fund such services out of his own pocket. At the same time, however, it should be emphasized that a number of the founding members devoted a great deal of volunteer time over a number of years. Hugo Beigel, for example, served as secretary, newsletter editor, and later, for many years, the Editor of *The Journal of Sex Research*. Robert V. Sherwin served as treasurer and membership chair and custodian of the Society's records. Later Leo Wollman served as secretary and newsletter editor.

Generally the new president took office at the end of the fall meeting, usually in November. In between annual conferences there were regular public meetings, and by January, 1963, there had been 21 such meetings. By this time, the *Newsletter* was several pages in length. Its contents included announcements, sex news and notes culled from both professional journals and the popular press, and book reviews, as well as news about individual members. The Newsletter became less important when *The Journal of Sex Research* began publication and, in fact, disappeared entirely for long stretches of time.

Activities of SSSS in its Early Years

All sexuality organizations owe a major debt to the founding group. Without its efforts, SIECUS, organized in 1964, would have had more difficulty than it did. In fact, many of the key figures in the SSSS were important to the formation of SIECUS which grew out of an informal discussion between Lester Kirkendall and Mary Calderone, both SSSS members. AASECT, organized in 1967, also has to look upon the SSSS as pioneering the field although the two organizations differed fundamentally over the certification of sex therapists. This issue was debated by the Society both before and after the founding of AASECT, and the refusal of the Society to certify individuals was an important factor in the growth of AASECT.

Although the SSSS always had members from outside the New York City area, for much of its early history it was regarded as primarily a New York City group. Most of its annual meetings and the regular quarterly meetings were held in New York City. One of the problems in going elsewhere was simply getting notices out about its meetings to nonmembers, a problem not solved until *The Journal of Sex Research* began to garner additional members and publicity. In its early years, the Society had great difficulty in publicizing its activities in other professional journals. The *Journal of the American Medical Association*, for example, refused to list meeting announcements of the Society in its regular columns. About the only means of publicity was by word of mouth, mailings, or paid announcements in the *Village Voice*, one of the few publications in New York City willing to accept advertisements about sex meetings. The Barbizon Plaza Hotel where the Society held many of its meetings even eliminated the word sex from the organization title, initially listing it as the Society for the Scientific Study and later simply as the SSSS. Ira Reiss, a charter member, and later president of the Society, indicated that it was difficult for non-New York City residents to attend and although he managed to do so when he taught at Bard College between 1959-1961, it was impossible for him to attend after moving to Iowa in 1961.

The Society's New York City base was both a strength and a weakness. It was a strength in that New York City had a critical mass of individuals who were interested enough in sex research not only to pay dues to a society but to attend meetings. Its weakness was the exclusion from participation (although not membership) of many of the major figures in sex research such as those associated with the Kinsey group (all of whom except for the by now deceased Kinsey joined) or the Masters and Johnson group, as well as others. Although publicity for meetings was undoubtedly a touchy subject, the Society seemingly was more hesitant to mention sex than it should have been, perhaps because of its initial experiences. In fact, until the 1980s, the initials of the Society, SSSS, continued to be used by the Society at its meetings rather than the full title. This perhaps added to the problem by implying (albeit unconsciously) that the society was doing something clandestine.

The Society, however, did not hesitate to deal with controversial subjects in both its annual meetings and in its more general ones. As mentioned above, this policy was initiated at the first conference at which one session was devoted to possible modifications in defining what was a therapeutic abortion. Other early conferences were devoted to an examination of religion and sex, artificial insemination (at this one the Nobel winner Herman Muller from Indiana University was in attendance and participated), interracial sex, sex problems of physicians and therapists, population control, pornography and psychology, advances in endocrinology, and other topics, many of them on the cutting edge of the field.

The Early Presidents

Ellis (1960-1962) was succeeded as president by Christopher Tietze (1962-1964). Tietze, a physician who had been forced to flee Austria, was at the

time of his election Research Director of the National Committee for Maternal Health, a position he later left to become a Senior Fellow in the Center for Policy Studies of the Population Council. Perhaps Tietze's major importance to the Society was in committing it early in its history to the proposition of reproductive choice, and in accepting the idea of use effectiveness – that is, experience with a contraceptive method or methods within a population in contrast to theoretical effectiveness or ineffectiveness under controlled laboratory conditions.

Hans Lehfeldt (1964-66), the third president, is an obstetrician and pioneer family planner, who has served the society in many capacities. Probably his most valuable service was in acting as a link between the pre-war sex groups and the original SSSS and between the founding members of the Society and later generations. He had attended the 1929 sex congress held in London and had retained contacts with some of the pioneer sexologists who had survived the Nazis. Of the original founding members, he has remained the one most intimately associated with the Society over the years and was still a member of the Board of Directors in the 1980s, at which time he was made Director Emeritus, a position he still holds.

The Journal of Sex Research

Collectively, the greatest accomplishment of the first three presidents and the other board members with whom they worked was inauguration of a journal, *The Journal of Sex Research*. At the first annual meeting in 1958, Lehfeldt reported that he and the other officers would concentrate their efforts

> on the publication of a scientific journal devoted to the various aspects of sex.... Now, having a Society with a nicely growing membership, we will redouble our efforts to produce such a journal.

As the first step, financial contributions were solicited from members and other interested individuals; some individuals also loaned money hoping to be paid back if the *Journal* was successful. Encouraged by this response the Society sponsored a Yearbook (Beigel, 1963), which included contributions by 31 members of the Society. Additional money was raised to issue a journal, and Vol. 1, No. 1 of *The Journal of Sex Research* appeared in March, 1965, during the presidency of Hans Lehfeldt. Most of the early contributions were invited and represented an international collection of individuals researching topics touching on human sexuality. Among the contributors to the first issue were Johann M. Burchard, MD, from Hamburg, West Germany; Valdemar Hartman, MSW, from the Forensic Clinic in the Department of Psychiatry at the University of Toronto; Karl Heinz Mehlan, MD, Director of the Institute for Hygiene at the University of Rostock; and Rudolf Peter, MD, director of the Third Obstetrical and Gynecological Clinic at the Charles University in Prague. Other contributors to the first volume from abroad included Roland Armijo, MD, and Tegualdo Monreal, MD, from the University of Chile in Santiago, Chile, and L.H. Levie from Amsterdam. American contributors to the first issue included John Money, PhD, from Johns Hopkins, former president Albert Ellis, the then president Hans Lehfeldt, Lili Peller, a psychoanalyst affiliated with the Department of Child Psychiatry of Einstein Medical College, and Hugo Beigel who was then retired from academic life and serving as Editor.

The second and third issues included contributions by past president Christopher Tietze, a multi-authored article by David A. Rodgers, PhD, and others, mostly from the Scripps Clinic and Research Foundation in LaJolla, CA; George Devereux, PhD, a Professor of Ethnopsychiatry at Temple University School of Medicine in Philadelphia; Harriet Pilpel, a prominent civil liberties attorney in New York City; Ofelia Mendoza, PhD, field director for the International Planned Parenthood Federation in New York City; Leo Wollman, MD, a gynecologist and psychotherapist in New York City; Wardell B. Pomeroy, PhD, then in private practice as a psychotherapist and marriage counselor in New York; Samuel Z. Klausner, from the Bureau of Social Science Research, in Washington, D.C.; Eugene Kanin, PhD, from the Department of Sociology at Purdue University; a multi-authored article on the sex offender in Minnesota by Nathan Mandel, PhD, from the Minnesota Department of Corrections, and others. Assisting Beigel as the Editor were five Associate Editors, Leo Chall, Albert Ellis, Henry Guze, George H. Liebmann, and Leo Wollman; Stephen Neiger and Conrad van Emde Boas were listed as Coeditors for Canada and the Netherlands respectively.

Some Problems

It is at this point in 1961 that I became acquainted with the Society and can testify first hand and use some of my own records to document what was taking place in the Society. A friend and colleague of mine, Mamoru Iga, was contacted by Hugo Beigel to do an article on prostitution in Japan, a subject on which I was then working. This was while the Journal was still in the planning stage and is indicative of the long range planning involved in the successful publication of the Journal. I immediately wrote requesting membership. As I remember it, and this is indicative of both the attitude of the Society and of society at large, the SSSS was fairly suspicious of me. I lived in California, claimed to be a historian, and was not known to anyone on the admissions committee. I also lacked a sponsor. After submitting various and assorted documents, I was accepted as a member but somehow it still took several years to get things straight, since periodically I did not get the *Journal*. In fact, for 2 years the Society lost track of me even though I was still living in the same house at the same address and teaching in the same institution.

My case was not unique. Marilyn Fithian, who later served as president of the Western Region, found that even though she had been receiving the *Journal* since 1965, had attended meetings and paid her dues, she had never been accepted into membership or, if she had, there was no official record of such an action. When she was elected president of the Western Region, she received a formal request to join the Society. These stories, and many similar ones reported to me, emphasize the difficulties the Society had in expanding. Obviously everyone in New York City had full-time jobs and the Society, even to that original group of dedicated volunteers, was secondary. Committees were mostly nonexistent. Some of the most overburdened individuals in the Society seemed unwilling to share responsibility. Inevitably, almost everything was brought to the Board, and a disproportionate amount of time at board meetings was occupied with membership applications or petty details, subjects that not all board members found interesting. Such problems are not unique to the Society but exist in a variety of voluntary organizations, both old and new, in many fields. In defense of these early workhorses, it has to be said that many of those from whom they requested help failed to deliver. Therefore, some of them grew increasingly reluctant to ask, feeling that since they probably would end up doing things themselves, they might as well just do them to begin with.

Inevitably many individuals burned out. Unfortunately, the task of dealing with the mundane details necessary to keep the Society alive seldom allowed them the time to devote to the larger issues for which they had founded the Society. Still the Society functioned and even grew. The 4th president of the society was Henry Guze (1966-1968), one of the founding members. He died in 1970. Guze was a pioneer in several fields and was one of the founders of the American Academy of Psychotherapists and the Society for Clinical and Experimental Hypnosis as well as the SSSS. He was succeeded by Wardell Pomeroy (1968-1970) who had been in clinical practice in New York City since 1963. Pomeroy was not only a coauthor of both of the early Kinsey volumes but also the sole author of several studies and a biography of Kinsey. During his presidency, Pomeroy made many of the initial contacts which ultimately led to the formation of the Western Region.

President Elect during Pomeroy's term was Sophia Kleegman, a prominent gynecologist who had been a student of the physician-sociologist, Robert Latou Dickinson. She also emphasized the continuous connection of the Society with its pioneer predecessors much as Lehfeldt and Ellis had done with the European and other sexologists. Due to illness, however, she could not take the presidency. As a result the Society did not have a woman executive officer for several more years. Kleegman died shortly after Richard Amelar, her candidate to replace her, took office as 6th president. Amelar (1970-1972), a New York City urologist specializing in male infertility problems, focused much of his research on human reproduction.

During Amelar's presidency the Society faced critical times. The initial enthusiasm of its founders was becoming more and more difficult to sustain as they continued to feel themselves overburdened with work. The Society was also hard hit by the growth of AASECT. The success of the AASECT certification program, regarded as essential by many of the therapists in the field, led many SSSS members to join with them. As indicated earlier, the SSSS had avoided this area after considerable debate because it did not feel it could control the services of the people it would be certifying. Still the challenge of AASECT forced a re-examination of the question, and the Society chose to continue to struggle as an organization whose purpose was the advancement of sex research rather than professional certification.

Western Region

The most important accomplishment of Amelar was the establishing of the Western Region. Pomeroy had made some initial efforts in this direction and Amelar continued them. The result was the organization of the Western Region with William Hartman, a sociologist at Long Beach State and perhaps best known as part of the Hartman and Fithian (Marilyn Fithian) team of sex therapists, serving as the first president. Initial meetings were held in the main dining room of a Chinese restaurant, forcing the meeting to be quite informal. The region soon began to hold regular quarterly dinner meetings at the "Tail of the Cock," at that time a prominent Los Angeles restaurant. The combination of the name of the restaurant and the subject matter of the Society made the meetings a kind of "in joke" among those who attended. For over a decade, the board meetings of the Western Region were held in the home of Julius and Naomi Winer.

Nationally, the most favorable result of the establishment of the Western Region was that it hosted the first national meeting outside of New York City. The 1972 meeting, held in Palm Springs, California, brought in not only a much needed infusion of funds but new members as well, giving the Society a second wind. The Society apparently had not fully thought through the implications of expansion because one unforeseen effect was the exclusion of Western Region members from any real say in the running of the Society. The Board continued to meet in New York City and few from outside the immediate New York area could afford to attend Board meetings. Thus the Board acted on purely New York City matters and on national matters at the same time serving both as a regional and a national Board. This problem of participation in national decision making plagued the Society for several years although occasionally either the Western Region or the Society itself was able to pay for the Western Board members to attend Board meetings. For a time there was also a SSSS group in Chicago, but it did not survive as a viable organization.

The Next Generation

SSSS Goes International

The Palm Springs meeting was the first national meeting of the Society which I attended, and this was true of most members on the west coast. It made me realize that the Society was more than a journal and that there were a large number of helpful and supportive people in the sex field. At that meeting there was further discussion over whether the SSSS should get into the certification field, but the decision once again was to stay out. Taking office as president-elect at the Palm Springs meeting was Jack Lippes (1972-1974), a Buffalo obstetrician specializing in reproductive physiology. He is perhaps best known for the "Lippes" loop. He was the first president from outside the New York City metropolitan area. It was under Lippes's leadership that groundwork was laid for the postwar revival of the kind of international sexological conferences held in the 20s and early 30s, and the Society not only gave leadership but provided some of the funds. By this time also, the Society had started a Fellows program and a number of people were made Fellows. As the Society grew, however, fewer individuals were designated Fellows as requirements became more stringent (See Appendix 3).

Carrying through on the initiatives of Lippes was the next president of the Society, John Money (1974-1976), the president who has written the most scientific papers on sexology – well over 300, along with numerous books. Under Money the Annual Meeting of the SSSS was merged with the first (Paris) and the second (Montreal) World Congresses of Sexology. This action not only was a major factor in launching the biennial world congresses but led to the founding of the World Association of Sexology (WAS). Money was a determined defender of sexology as a science, emphasizing both the need for political vigilance and political action regarding legislation destructive of sexology. By the time Money was president, the Society had grown enough and was wealthy enough to hire its first paid administrative assistant, Mary Westervelt; her husband, Frank, assisted her. This helped the Society become somewhat more administratively efficient.

Money also took steps to establish a 1-term presidency, and it was with this assumption that the next president, Richard Green (1976-1978) took office. Green earlier had expressed disappointment with the caliber of research being reported in *The Journal of Sex Research*, a criticism also made by others. Part of the difficulty was that Beigel, the Editor, almost singlehandedly selected material and handled all administrative duties, and he was concerned more with being original and provocative than with publishing refereed articles reporting research. Green's disappointment ultimately led him to found the *Archives of Sexual Behavior* in association with Plenum Press. This meant that *The Journal of Sex Research* was no longer alone in the field and, if the Society was to grow and expand, it was important to meet this new challenge. There was also a new organization associated with the *Archives*, the International Academy of Sex Research. The founding of the *Archives* was significant primarily because Plenum Press was breaking new ground in publishing journals in specialized areas where it felt there was untapped market potential. Sex research, previously regarded as somewhat stigmatized, obviously was no longer so regarded. If its articles were to be accepted as authoritative, it was imperative that the *Journal* establish more rigorous criteria for publication. At the same time the Society itself had to rethink what it was doing.

Virginia Johnson had been elected as president-elect to succeed Green, but she resigned her position before taking office. Green was persuaded to remain for a second term. The resignation of Johnson, the internationally known partner in the Masters and Johnson team, meant that once again the Society was delayed in having a woman as president.

Organizationally, the SSSS, in spite of the efforts of the Westervelts to systematize the day to day administration, remained rather informal. Clive Davis, for example, first became a Board member because he attended an 8 a.m. business meeting in Montreal in 1976 and, after being introduced, found himself nominated and elected to the Board. Essentially, what was taking place in the SSSS was a kind of changing of the guard, aided and abetted by the demands of the Western Region. The original founders who had dedicated so much of their time and energy to the organization were, for the most part, no longer in leadership positions. Moreover, because much of the initial financing came from the SSSS, the efforts to expand the sexological movement to Europe, had in the short run proved financially draining to the Society. In addition, because the annual conferences of the Society were an important source of income, the failure to hold annual meetings in the years in which the International Congresses were held added to the problem, making the drain a hemorrhage.

Changing of the Guard

Perhaps because of these problems, Green's presidency seems to coincide with the major changes in the nature of the Society. Beigel, who had given so much of his time and energy to the *Journal*, had become ill in early 1977. John Money had taken over the editorship for the second issue of Volume 13, and, by the third issue Clive Davis had been appointed his successor. An Eastern Region was also organized with Jerome Zoppo as president, Betty Stassi, vice president, Connie Christine (Tina) Wheeler as treasurer, and Robert Francoeur as secretary. The Western Region had also made a major contribution to restoring the coffers of the society by hosting the 20th annual meeting in Las Vegas, Nevada, October 28-30, 1977. In 1978, the Society, however, participated as usual at the third International Congress of Sexology in Rome.

Leah Schaefer (1978-1979), the 10th president, was the first woman to serve in that office, and the first person to serve the new 1-year term. Long known for her work with transvestites and transsexuals, Schaefer made a special effort to incorporate a large number of individuals who had previously not been active in the Society into positions of responsibility. She resolved some of the continuing conflict between the Society's New York City base and its outlying regions by appointing some committee chairpersons from outside New York City, and to make them further functional she put a majority of members on these same committees from the chair's geographical region so that meetings could be held and problems worked on during the year through face to face contact as well as by letter with those members who lived in other areas of the country. Still, a proposed policy of paying transportation for Western Region Board members to attend a Board meeting would soon have bankrupted the organization. The problem was that much of the financial strength of the SSSS lay in the Western Region, but this group was cut off from effective decision making in the organization. One way to deal with this was to build up an effective Eastern Region, separate and distinct from the national, and Schaefer concentrated on this. Under Schaefer, Connie Christine (Tina) Wheeler served as a part- time Executive Director of the Society, an important concept, but one which in the short run proved financially disastrous. What this appointment did was to separate the day to day tasks of the Society which were carried out by the Westervelts in Glen Burnie, Maryland, from the larger issues of administration and policy which were under the direction of Wheeler and Schaefer. Under Schaefer also, steps were taken to reinvigorate the newsletter, which for a short period had ceased regular publication.

Succeeding Schaefer as president was William Hartman (1979-1980), the first westerner to become president. Hartman found that the Society was in very poor economic condition and on the verge of bankruptcy. Under his leadership the position held by Wheeler was abolished in order to curtail expenses, and the Society adopted an annual budget with realistic expectations of anticipated income and outgo. Some indication of the burdens placed on a president was the fact that Hartman found he had to assign a full-time secretary from his own office staff to handle Society business, in spite of the support services given by the Westervelts.

Taking place simultaneously and independently during Hartman's presidency was the organization of an informal long-range planning session called together by John Sumerlin, then president of the Eastern Region. This was the first long-range planning group of any kind since the informal organizational meetings when the Society was founded. Among those attending, besides Schaefer and Sumerlin, were several future presidents of the SSSS including Elizabeth Allgeier, Clive Davis, Vern Bullough, Donald Mosher. One result was the establishment of an informal agenda outlining future goals and objectives. Ultimately, in the course of the next few years, the agenda adopted by the group was implemented. Adding to the pace of change was the necessity of replacing the retiring Westervelts and here, the next president, Ira Reiss (1980-1981) took the dominant role.

Professionalizing the Organization of the Society

Reiss, the possessor of strong organizational skills as well as a reputation as a distinguished sex researcher, led a national search for a new full-time Executive Director combining the jobs held by the Westervelts plus those previously carried out on a part-time and often volunteer basis by Tina Wheeler. Reiss persuaded the Board that the headquarters of the Society could move to wherever the new Executive Director lived, and when, Deborah Weinstein was chosen, Philadelphia became the new head-quarters. With the establishment of a new paid full-time Executive Direc-tor, the nature of the presidency of the Society began to change. Increasingly the day-to-day burdens of running the Society were trans-ferred to her. During this period the Society also withdrew financial backing from the WAS-sponsored Washington D. C. World Congress. One reason for this was the tight budget which the SSSS had adopted for itself, but a more significant reason was disagreement by SSSS repre-sentatives with the way both financial and planning arrangements were being handled by the WAS planning committee.

The full effect of the changes in SSSS, particularly the appointment of a full-time Executive Director, was felt under the succeeding presidents, of which I was the first. I served two 1-year terms (1981-1983) because the Society was in the midst of a transition, and there was a reluctance to change presidents after 1 year. Later the constitution was amended so that such an occurrence would be much less likely in the future. My experience on professional boards matched Reiss's and following the work of my predecessors, I was able to bring about a basic change in the nature of the way the Board conducted its business.

With the aid of Executive Director Weinstein, the committee structure, initially established by Schaefer on a national level, was expanded, a Midcontinent Region was organized, and the Western Region was ex-tended beyond its Los Angeles base. The first president of the Midcon-tinent Region was Howard J. Ruppel, Jr. Robert Birch was treasurer and Sue Hammersmith was secretary.

Steps were taken to downsize the Board and limitations were put on terms. Although final decision making remained with the Board, most of the agenda items were reports of committees. The Society Newsletter which had been revived under the editorship of Andrew Behrendt, was regularized. A directory of members was published. Subscriptions to some of the other professional sex journals were arranged at a discount, the foundation was laid for an accrediting process of institutions with either degree or special certificate programs in human sexuality, and cooperative agreements were worked out between AASECT, SIECUS, and other sexuality organizations.

Cooperation with Other Sex Organizations and the Establishment of the Foundation

One result of this cooperative spirit was a special combined SSSS/AASECT Annual Meeting taking place under the presidency of Joseph LoPiccolo (1983-1984), a distinguished psychologist known for his research in the area of sexual dysfunction and numerous other aspects of human sexuality. It was under LoPiccolo's presidency that the Society again became debt free and financially stable. The membership continued to grow dramatically. Under LoPiccolo it was also agreed that the Society's archives which had been expanded by Leah Schaefer were to be transferred to the Kinsey Institute.

LoPiccolo was succeeded by Clive Davis (1984-85) who was best known in the field for his editorship of *The Journal of Sex Research*, which he had upgraded to a first class journal. As president, Davis' greatest accomplishment was in establishing The Foundation for the Scientific Study of Sexuality, which under his leadership was incorporated as a separate nonprofit and tax exempt foundation. This action emphasizes the growing financial and professional success of the Society that had been near bankruptcy in 1980. (See page ii for the Mission Statement of FSSS and Appendix 5 for a list of the Founding Donors and Board of Directors.) The Society's awards were restructured in 1985 with the renaming of the annual award as the Award for Distinguished Scientific Achievement and the creation of the awards for Distinguished Service to SSSS and Public Service. (See Appendix 4 for a list of the Society's Awards and their recipients.)

Davis was succeeded by Elizabeth Allgeier (1985-1986), perhaps best known for her college textbook in the field of human sexuality. Allgeier continued to involve ever more members in the running of the Society, and under her leadership, the Society became an affiliate of the American Association for the Advancement of Science. Since the practice of designating editors for 5-year terms had been set by the publication committee earlier, Allgeier's presidency also coincided with another notable changing of the guard when a selection committee for a new *Journal* Editor began working. Plans were also made to extend southward and hold the SSSS's first Annual Meeting in the southeast.

Allgeier was succeeded by David McWhirter (1986-1987), the first physician to be president since Richard Green, emphasizing the continuing interdisciplinary nature of the Society. McWhirter was also from the West (although with eastern ties) and the first publicly out of the closet gay person to be president of the Society. A researcher into gay relationships, McWhirter had the honor of presiding over the 30th anniversary meeting of the Society and with Davis was instrumental in establishing the tradition of an annual fund-raising dinner. He established a Task Force on AIDS, helped complete the transition to a new *JSR* editor, Paul R. Abramson, and extended the scientific content of meetings.

Marking the 31st year of the Society as president was Donald Mosher (1987-1988) whose term took the Society in new directions. As founder of the Committee on Scientific and Professional Affairs (COSPA), Mosher had taken the initiative in the Society's response to the Attorney General's Committee on Pornography, established SSSS liaison with the American Civil Liberties Union, emphasized the professionalization of sex research and the need for the Society to take public stands on issues on which Society members had expertise.

Conclusion

In looking back over the past 30 years, there has been a remarkable change in public attitudes toward research into sexuality. The Society has been both a factor in bringing about these changes and has benefited from them. A number of reasons can be advanced for the changes that took place. One obvious reason is that the second wave of feminism, beginning in the 1950s, demanded changes in the sexist attitudes of society. Helping to fuel the debate for changes was the opportunity of women for greater reproductive freedom, a direct result of sex research. New contraceptive methods such as Lippes loop and oral contraceptives, developments in which Society members played a part, were significant factors in providing women greater sexual independence. The availability of legal abortion, a question with which the Society wrestled in its first annual meeting, also significantly contributed to greater freedom. In terms of female sexuality, the pioneering work of William Masters and Virginia Johnson allowed women to publicly express themselves as sexual creatures (Masters & Johnson, 1966, 1970).

Members of the Society also played a significant role in reassessing the role of pornography ("Report," 1970), a project which had been initiated by President Lyndon Johnson. The more recent report issued by the U.S. Attorney General's office had less input from Society members and as a result managed to ignore most research in the area of human sexuality. Without the new attitudes toward pornography, accentuated by the first report, it would not have been possible for therapists to use many of the films now available to help their clients. In fact, the whole field of sexual therapy was pioneered during the period of the Society's existence by William Masters, Virginia Johnson, William Hartman, Marilyn Fithian, and others.

Traditionally stigmatized behavior has also come out in the open and in the process become somewhat less stigmatized. Homosexuality which had been classified as a form of mental illness or developmental deficit by psychoanalysts such as Irving Bieber and Edmund Bergler and non-psychoanalysts such as C. Allen, G.W. Henry and numerous others (Allen, 1949; Bergler, 1956; Bieber, Dain, & Dince, 1962, and Henry, 1941) was removed from the illness category by the American Psychiatric Association in 1974. One reason for this was research demonstrating that such an assumption was not valid. Individuals associated with the Society also pioneered in giving new insight into transvestism, transsexualism and various forms of gender dysphoria (Benjamin, 1966; Green & Money, 1969). All forms of sexual behavior were open to examination and re-searchers now consider physiological, psychological, social, cultural and historical aspects of sexuality.

Obviously research alone did not bring about changes in society, but the results were seized upon by previously excluded groups such as women, gays, lesbians, transvestites, and transsexuals, arguing for a new basis for their existence. Using research findings, they were able to campaign for changes, and, in the process, the Society itself could come out of the closet, no longer simply listed as SSSS but as the Society for the Scientific Study of Sex. Today, it seems doubtful that anyone at a major university would be dismissed for saying what Koch did in the year the Society was founded.

The connection between research and public policy is important, and it is this direction that Donald Mosher has been encouraging the Society to move. The debate over the spread of AIDS, the radical feminist inter-pretation of the dangers of pornography, and the anti-abortion agitation all indicate that viewpoints differ between large segments of society and the majority of Society members. Obviously, research into sexuality in all its aspects is just beginning, but it is expanding at a significant rate, and many of the traditional disciplines such as my own, history, are eager and willing to accept research articles on sexuality. In fact, in recent years I have published a number of updated versions of articles on sexuality in historical journals that at one time were sent back to me unread because of the nature of the subject matter (i.e., sex).

We still do not have an adequate sex education program in this country; we do not deal very effectively with sexually transmitted diseases; sexual problems are still a major issue in many marriages and other long term relationships; adult-child sexual interactions remain relatively unexplored; the ground has barely been broken on gender dysphoria issues; en-docrinology studies have just touched the surface; the relationship be-tween a culture and its sexual attitudes needs more investigation; and after centuries of physiological studies, we are just beginning to understand the problems of impotence and the nonorgasmic women. The list could go on since there are many aspects of sexology about which we still know little.

One of the difficulties with some of the current research is the over reliance upon college students as research subjects, a good pool for some topics but not for others. Still, the level of research has risen considerably in the last 30 years as evidenced by an examination of the pages of *The Journal of Sex Research*, the *Archives of Sex Behavior*, the *Journal of Homosexuality*, or any of the numerous other journals recently entering the field. The Society is positioned well to take a leadership role in the future, but, to do so, it must continue to expand its base. Its advantage has always been the interdisciplinary nature of the membership, and, in the sex field, this multidisciplinary approach is all important. However, this type of research, whether by an individual or a team, requires special efforts to maintain communication. It is essential that the members from the different and sometimes competing disciplines and professions speak and understand the same language of sexology. It also demands that each of us leave the security of our disciplinary expertise. This can be a frightening experience to those first experiencing it.

The Society has managed to survive 3 decades. As it enters the 4th it is stronger than ever and has a strong grass roots base. Perhaps the best illustration of the growth is in looking at the paraphernalia accumulated by the Society. The original administrator of the SSSS was Robert Sherwin who ran it out of a file drawer in his office. When Sherwin was succeeded by Charles Ihlenfeld, there was only one file box of records and memberships. When Mary and Frank Westervelt took over as administrators in Glen Burnie, Maryland, Ihlenfeld transferred two shopping bags of materials pertaining to the members and the Society. In 1981, when the Westervelts retired and Deborah Weinstein was hired as Executive Director, the records of the Society had grown to four filing cabinets plus back issues of the *Journal of Sex Research*, a worktable, and an adding machine. The Society had not yet acquired a typewriter, let alone a computer, or considered establishing an archives. When the SSSS moved to Iowa in 1988, where the new Executive Director, Howard Ruppel, made his home, it needed a good sized van. There was not only a computer and the paraphernalia associated with it, many filing cases, and annual case books, but there was also an independent archive collection in Indiana which was not transported in the van, and the back issues of the *Journal* were available from a commercial source and no longer moved from office to office. Although the Society has not yet joined the ranks of such organizations as the American Medical Association in having its own building, it seems to have become a well-established learned and professional society. The key words are *seem to* because in order to preserve its status as the grandmother of the current group of societies and groups dealing with human sexuality, it is essential it keep serving its members and extend its services. It has given birth, in one way or another, to SIECUS, AASECT, SSTAR, the International Academy, the World Congress, and other organizations. Though some of the offspring have been fairly rebellious, and AASECT is larger, the SSSS remains a strong grass-roots interdisciplinary organization. When all is said and done that is what the professional society should be.

In spite of all the progress, the SSSS members are professionals in a field remaining somewhat stigmatized, although few doubt the importance of a better understanding of human sexuality. Probably, for that reason, its members have always felt that they cannot ignore what takes place in society around them. Though there was always a dichotomy in sex research between the sex reformers and the sex researchers, the Society has so far been able to emphasize the importance of trying to give society the information about what its members know. Some of this is done by the sex educators and popularizers holding membership in the Society; some through publications. Still the Board of the Society, as well as many of its members, have found it important to take stands on many of the sexual issues facing society in general. When this occurs, as in the case of pornography, AIDS, or other issues, there is always a strong effort to put such stands in the context of the research. What the Society seems to do best is to bring two strands of the past together, the reformers and researchers, and to emphasize that researchers need not confine their findings to unread monographs and journal articles. By emphasizing both the methods of research and the findings of the researchers, the Society for the Scientific Study of Sex may also furnish the data for effective public understanding.

References

Allen, C. (1949). *The sexual perversions and abnormalities*. London: Oxford University Press.

American Association of University Professors Bulletin. (1963, March). *49*, pp. 25-43.

Beigel, H. (1963). (Ed.). *Advances in sex research*. New York: Harper & Row.

Bergler, E. (1956). *Homosexuality*. New York: Hill and Wang.

Bieber, I., Dain, H.J., & Dince, A.R. (1962). *Homosexuality*. New York: Basic Books.

Broderick, C.B. (1988). To arrive where we started: The field of family studies in the 1930's. *Journal of Marriage and Family, 50*, 569-584.

Bullough, V.L. (1976). *Sexual variance in society and history*. Chicago: University of Chicago Press.

Bullough, V.L. (1980). Technology and female sexuality. *The Journal of Sex Research, 16*, 59-71.

Bullough, V.L. (1981). A brief note on rubber technology: The diaphragm and the condom. *Technology and Culture, 22*, 104-111.

Bullough, V.L. (1985a). The Rockefellers and sex research. *The Journal of Sex Research, 21*, 113-125.

Bullough, V.L. (1985b). Merchandising the sanitary napkin. *Signs, 10*, 615-627.

Bullough, V.L. (1987, December). *Homosexuality and sex research*. Paper presented at the Congress, Homosexuality Beyond Disease, Amsterdam, The Netherlands. (Proceedings will be published.)

Bullough, V.L. (1988a). Katherine Bement Davis, sex research, and the Rockefeller Foundation. *Bulletin of the History of Medicine, 62*, 74-89.

Bullough, V.L. (1988b, May 5). The physician and sex research. The Garrison Lecture, American Association for the History of Medicine, New Orleans. Paper will be published in the *Bulletin of the History of Medicine*.

Bullough, V.L., & Voght, M. (1973). Women, menstruation, and nineteenth century medicine. *Bulletin of the History of Medicine*, *47*, 66-82.

Bullough, V.L., Shelton, B., & Slavin, S. (1988). *The subordinated sex.* Athens, Ga.: University of Georgia Press.

Dickinson, R.L., & Beam, L. (1931). *A thousand marriages: A medical study of sex adjustment.* Baltimore: Williams and Wilkins. Introduction by Havelock Ellis.

Dickinson, R.L., & Beam, L. (1949). *The single woman: A medical study in sex education.* Baltimore: Williams and Wilkins.

Davis, K.B. (1929). *Factors in the sex life of twenty-two hundred women.* New York: Harper and Brothers.

Ellis, A. (1951). *Folklore of Sex.* New York: C. Boni.

Ellis, A. (1951, 1952). *Sex beliefs and customs.* London: P. Nevill.

Ellis, H. (1936). *Studies in the psychology of sex* (Vol. 2). New York: Modern Library.

Hamilton, G.V. (1929). *A research in marriage.* New York: A.C. Boni.

Henry, G.W. (1944). *Sex variants.* New York: Hoeber.

Kinsey, A.C., Pomeroy, W.B., & Martin, C.E. (1948). *Sexual behavior in the human male.* Philadelphia: W.B. Saunders.

Kinsey, A.C., Pomeroy, W.B., Martin, C. E., & Gebhard, P. (1953). *Sexual behavior in the human female.* Philadelphia: W.B. Saunders.

Krafft-Ebing, Richard von. (1894). *Psychopathia sexualis* (7th ed). (C.G. Chaddock, Trans.). Philadelphia: F.A. Davis.

Masters, W.H., & Johnson, V.E. (1966). *Human sexual response.* Boston: Little Brown.

Masters, W.H., & Johnson, V.E. (1970). *Human sexual inadequacy.* Boston: Little Brown.

Parent-Duchatlet, A.J.P. (1837). *De la prostitution dans la ville de Paris [Prostitution in the City of Paris] (Vols. l-2) (2nd ed.).* Paris: J.B. Bailliere.

Pearson, K. (1888). *The ethic of free thought.* London: T. Fisher Unwin.

Report of the Commission on Obscenity and Pornography. (1970). Washington, D.C.: U. S. Government Printing Office.

Thurston, F. M. (1932). *A bibliography on family relationships.* New York: National Council of Parent Education.

Appendix 1

Past presidents and their terms of office

Albert Ellis (1960-1962)

Christopher Tietze (1962-1964)

Hans Lehfeldt (1964-1966)

Henry Guze (1966-1968)

Wardell Pomeroy (1968-1970)

Richard Amelar (1970-1972)

Jack Lippes (1972-1974)

John Money (1974-1976)

Richard Green (1976-1978)

Leah Schaefer (1978-1979)

William Hartman (1979-1980)

Ira L. Reiss (1980-1981)

Vern L. Bullough (1981-1983)

Joseph LoPiccolo (1983-1984)

Clive M. Davis (1984-1985)

Elizabeth R. Allgeier (1985-1986)

David McWhirter (1986-1987)

Donald L. Mosher (1987-1988)

Kenneth D. George (1988-1989)

Eli Coleman (President-Elect) (1989-1990)

Presidents of SSSS Regions

Eastern Region

Jerome Zoppo
Leo Wollman
John Sumerlin
Leah Cahan Schaefer
Kenneth D. George
Robert T. Francoeur
Konstance McCaffree

Midcontinent Region

Howard J. Ruppel, Jr.
Frank Farley
Sue K. Hammersmith
Eli Coleman
Marilyn Story
Barbara Wiedemann Ruppel

Western Region

William E. Hartman
George R. Bach
Julius H. Winer
Alex Runciman
Marilyn Fithian
Harvey Cantor
Robert Reitman
J. Jones Stewart
Thomas Logan

Rebecca Black
David McWhirter
Dwight Dixon
Veronica D. Elias
Milton Diamond
Bernard Goldstein
Peter T. Knoepfler
Pepper Schwartz

Appendix 2

Charter Members of the Society for the Scientific Study of Sex

Hugo Beigel, Ph.D.

Harry Benjamin, M.D.

Conrad van Emde Boas, M.D.

Ewald Bohm, Ph.D.

Fred Brown, Ph.D.

Leo P. Chall, Ph.D.

LeMon Clark, M.D.

Robert C. Cook

George W. Corner, M.D.

Lester W. Dearborn

Winston W. Ehrmann, Ph.D.

Albert Ellis, Ph.D.

Vernon W. Grant, Ph.D.

J. P. Greenhill, M.D.

Max Gruenthal, M.D.

Henry Guze, Ph.D.

M. A. Hai, M.D.

Robert A. Harper, Ph.D.

L. Clovis Hirning, M.D.

Edwin Hirsch, M.D.

Edward J. Humphreys, M.D.

Arnold H. Kegel, M.D.

G. Lombard Kelly, M.D.

Lester Kirkendall, Ph.D.

Sophia J. Kleegman, M.D.

Ernest W. Kulka, M.D.

Herbert S. Kupperman, Ph.D., M.D.

Hans Lehfeldt, M.D.

Milton I. Levine, M.D.

David R. Mace, Ph.D.

H.S. Mehta, F.C.P.S.

John Money, Ph.D.

George P. Murdock, Ph.D.

Gottfried Neumann, M.D.

Harriet Pilpel, Ll.B.

Morris Ploscowe, Judge

Sandor Rado, M.D.

Glenn Ramsey, Ed.D.

B. Krishna Rao, M.B., B.S.

Ira L. Reiss, Ph.D.

Harold Rosen, M.D.

I. C. Rubin, M.D.

Robert Veit Sherwin, L.L.B.

Meyer Solomon, M.D.

Walter Stokes, M.D.

Christopher Tietze, M.D.

William Vogt, Sc.D.

Appendix 3

Society Fellows

Fellows are elected for outstanding contributions to the sphere of sexual knowledge. Election is by the Board of Directors upon recommendation of the Fellows Committee. Members may apply on their own initiative or may be invited to apply by the Fellows Committee or by members of the Board.

Paul Abramson, Ph.D.
Elizabeth Rice Allgeier, Ph.D.
Ben Ard, Ph.D.
Margaret Bowers, M.D.
Bonnie Bullough, Ph.D., R.N.
Vern L. Bullough, Ph.D., R.N.
Donn Byrne, Ph.D.
Edward Brecher
Mary Calderone, M.D.
Eli Coleman, Ph.D.
Clive M. Davis, Ph.D.
Edward Dengrove, M. D.
Milton Diamond, Ph.D.
Anke Ehrhardt, Ph.D.
Albert Ellis, Ph.D.
Carol Rinkleib Ellison, Ph.D.
William Fisher, Ph.D.
Marilyn Fithian, B.A.
Robert T. Francoeur, Ph.D.
Matthew Freund, Ph.D.
Paul Gebhard, Ph.D.
Kenneth George, Ed.D
Richard Green, M.D.
Erwin Haeberle, Ph.D.
Robert Harper, Ph.D.
Julia Heiman, Ph.D.
Preben Hertoft, M.D.
Janet S. Hyde, Ph.D.
Virginia Johnson, M.A.
Sherwin Kaufman, M.A.
Lester Kirkendall, Ph.D.
Robert Kolodny, M. D.
Stanley Krippner, Ph.D.
Anthony Labrum, M.D.
Hans Lehfeldt, M.D.

Sandra Leiblum, Ph.D.
Leo Levie, M.D.
Harold Lief, M.D.
Roger Libby, Ph.D.
Joseph LoPiccolo, Ph.D.
Floyd Martinson, Ph.D.
William Masters, M.D.
Tom Mazur, Psy.D.
David McWhirter, M.D.
Heino Meyer-Bahlburg, Dr.rer.nat.
John Money, Ph.D.
Donald L. Mosher, Ph.D.
Emily Mudd, Ph.D.
Willy Pasini, M.D.
Wardell Pomeroy, Ph.D.
Ira L. Reiss, Ph.D.
June M. Reinisch, Ph.D.
Robert Reitman, Ph.D.
Raymond Rosen, Ph.D.
Sharon Satterfield, M.D.
Leah C. Schaefer, Ed.D.
James Semans, Ph.D.
Hirsch Silverman, M.D.
Laura Singer, Ed.D.
James Sobrino, Ph.D.
William Stayton, Th.D.
J. Jones Stewart, M.D.
Walter Stokes, M.D., L.L.B.
Clayton Thomas, Ph.D.
Bruce Voeller, Ph.D.
Douglas Wallace, Ph.D.
David Weis, Ph.D.
Mary Westervelt
Christine Wheeler

Appendix 4

Society Award Recipients

Recipients of SSSS Award for Distinguished Scientific Achievement

John Bancroft, M.D.	Harry Harlow, Ph.D.
Frank Beach, Ph.D.	Carl Hartman, M.D.
Harry Benjamin, M.D.	Virginia Johnson, M.A.
Donn Byrne, Ph.D.	Robert Kolodny, M.D.
Mary Calderone, M.D.	Hans Lehfeldt, M.D.
George W. Corner, M.D.	Harold Lief, M.D.
Albert Ellis, Ph.D.	William Masters, M.D.
John Gagnon, Ph.D.	John Money, Ph.D.
Paul Gebhard, Ph.D.	Wardell B. Pomeroy, Ph.D.
Allan Guttmacher, M.D.	Jan Raboch, Dr.Sc.
Richard Green, M.D.	Ira L. Reiss, Ph.D.
Henry Guze, M.D.	William Simon, Ph.D.

Recipients of Distinguished Service to SSSS Award

The Distinguished Service Award for service to the SSSS was instituted in 1985. The award is granted to a member of the Society in recognition of outstanding and extensive service to the organization.

Leah C. Schaefer, Ed.D., 1985

Clive M. Davis, Ph.D., 1987

Deborah Weinstein, M.S.W. 1988

Recipients of Public Service Award

Established in 1985, the SSSS Public Service Award is given to individuals for outstanding achievement or major impact in such areas as public awareness of sexual issues, public advocacy, professional practice by educators, therapists, or health specialists, and legislation or public policy formation.

Bill Baird, 1985

Harriet Pilpel, L.L.B., 1987

Michael Barrett, Ph.D., 1989

SSSS Student Research Grant Recipients

The Society's Student Research Program grants an annual award of $500 to graduate students conducting research in the area of human sexuality.

Ilsa Lottes, 1985

Mary A. Koralewski, 1986

Kristen L. Rowe, 1987

Cudore L. Snell, 1988

Vince A.F. Salazar, 1989

Hugo C. Beigel Research Award Recipients

This prestigious award is named in memory of Hugo G. Beigel, a founding member of SSSS and Editor of *The Journal of Sex Research* for 13 years. The award is designed to promote and to reward research excellence in sexology; the recipient is the author of the best article published each year in the *Journal.*

Donald L. Mosher, Ph.D. and Barbara White, 1981

Michael Ross, Ph. D., 1982

Victor Malatesta, Ph.D., Robert Pollack, Ph.D.,

Terri Crotty, Ph.D. and Lelon J. Peacock, Ph.D., 1983

David Weis, Ph.D., 1984

Bernard Apfelbaum, Ph.D., 1985

Barry Singer, Ph.D., 1986

Richard C. Pillard, M.D. and James D. Weinrich, Ph.D., 1987

Beverly Whipple, Ph.D. and Barry R. Komisaruk, Ph.D., 1988

FSSS Board of Directors

1989

Clive M. Davis, Ph.D., President

Theodore Casparian, Vice-President

Maria Flaherty, Ph.D., Secretary

Rebecca Black, M.A., Treasurer

Members-at-Large

Elizabeth Rice Allgeier, Ph.D.

Veronica D. Elias, Ph.D.

Frank Farley, Ph.D.

Floyd M. Martinson, Ph.D.

Leah C. Schaefer

James D. Weinrich, Ph.D.

Edward L. Anderson, Ph.D.

Robert Embree, Ph.D.

Kenneth D. George, Ed.D.

Donald L. Mosher, Ph.D.

Howard J. Ruppel, Jr., M.A.

Deborah Weinstein, M.S.W.

Naomi Winer

Executive Director

Howard J. Ruppel, Jr., M.A.

FSSS Founding Donors

Elizabeth Rice Allgeier
Edward L. Anderson
Rebecca Black
Rupert R. Brook
F. Robert Brush
Vern L. & Bonnie Bullough
Harvey Cantor
Eli Coleman
Richard J. Cross
J. Kenneth Davidson
Clive M. & Sandra L. Davis
Veronica D. & James E. Elias
Robert Embree

Frank Farley
Charles L. Ihlenfeld
Floyd M. Martinson
David P. McWhirter &
Andrew M. Mattison
Ronald Moglia &
Ann Welbourne-Moglia
Donald L. Mosher &
Susan B. Bond
Howard J. &
Barbara W. Ruppel
Jack Spund
Deborah Weinstein

President's Circle of Donors

Naomi Winer

Directors' Guild of Donors

Theodore & Elizabeth M. Casparian

James & Betty Ramey

John E. Dopyera

Robert J. Greenwald

James Weinrich